ROBERT
the BRUCE

The Young Knight

ROBERT THE BRUCE was born into the nobility in 1274. The Bruce family were descended from Adam de Brus, who had crossed over from Normandy with William the Conqueror. William had given de Brus lands in Yorkshire and the family had later acquired land in Huntingdonshire and in Annandale, Scotland. There are no records of Bruce's early years, but some things can be deduced from his later exploits.

He could speak at least three languages – Gaelic (learned from his mother's people in Carrick), Norman-French (the language of the aristocracy) and northern English (spoken by the lowland Scots of Annandale). He lived at Turnberry but must often have visited his grandfather, who occupied the family seat at Lochmaben in Annandale. The young Robert clearly became very familiar with the wild countryside between the two castles. Finally, since he was later ranked as one of the three best knights in Christendom, he must have learned well the skills of knighthood – the use of weapons and horse-riding.

Although the Bruces owed allegiance to Edward I, the king of England, for their English lands, and to Alexander III, the king of Scotland, for their lands in Annandale, there was no conflict of loyalties while the two kingdoms remained at peace. In 1286, however, when Bruce was 11 years old, Alexander died, leaving his granddaughter Margaret, a young girl in Norway, as his only direct heir. Alexander's reign was later regarded as a golden age: the country was prosperous and there had been peace with England for nearly 100 years. While Scotland had a strong king, Edward had been content to respect his neighbour's independence, but now, seeing his chance to gain control in Scotland, he proposed that his son Edward marry 'the Maid of Norway'. The Scots agreed but only on the conditions spelt out in the Treaty of Birgham of 1290, that Edward recognize the separateness and independence of the Scottish nation. Edward agreed, but the Maid of Norway died in September 1290.

TURNBERRY CASTLE
Robert the Bruce was born on 11 July 1274 in Turnberry Castle in Carrick, on the south-west coast of Scotland. The castle was built to be impregnable from the sea.

MAID OF NORWAY
On her way from Norway to Scotland, Margaret – the Maid of Norway – became ill and died in Orkney. Alexander III's children having died before him, there was now no clear successor to the Scottish throne.

LOCHMABEN CASTLE

Lochmaben in Annandale was the seat of the Bruce family in Scotland. During Robert's childhood, his grandfather, known as Robert the Competitor, lived at Lochmaben and the young Robert would often have ridden over to see him. The castle shown here was built during the early 1300s.

LORD OF ANNANDALE

The coat of arms of the Bruce family in Annandale. Family loyalty and affection were strong among the Bruces: they passionately supported the family's claim to the throne and, later, Bruce's brothers and sisters endured unbelievable hardships on his behalf.

. Robert de brus'

FEUDAL LOYALTIES

Under the feudal system, the king held his kingdom directly from God, the supreme overlord. The king granted land to his nobles and knights who therefore owed him fealty (an oath of homage in which they swore loyalty). Each knight further subdivided his land to tenants or vassals, who in return swore fealty and promised to provide warriors to fight for the knight – and the king – when required.

SCOTLAND IN THE 13TH CENTURY

This map was drawn c.1250 by Matthew Paris, a monk of St Albans. It is part of one of the earliest detailed maps of Great Britain but shows little knowledge of Scotland beyond the coast and rivers.

Family Ambitions

THE DEATH of the Maid of Norway left no clear successor, but many contenders, to the Scottish throne, including Bruce's grandfather, Robert the Competitor. His was one of the two strongest claims based on descent from David, the brother of an earlier Scottish king, William I. Robert the Competitor was the son of David's second daughter and John Balliol was the grandson of David's eldest daughter. The Scots asked Edward I to decide who had the better claim.

Edward's court pronounced in favour of John Balliol, who was enthroned as king in November 1292. The Bruces, including Robert, who was now 18 years old, never accepted this decision: they refused to pay homage to John Balliol and swore fealty only to Edward I. Robert the Competitor retired to Lochmaben and died there in April 1295, while Robert's father went to Norway where he stayed until he was appointed Governor of Carlisle in 1295. Robert the Bruce became Earl of Carrick and head of the family in Scotland.

Meanwhile things were not going well for John Balliol. In 1293, Edward declared the Treaty of Birgham null and void and left King John with so little power he was nick-named Toom Tabard, 'the Empty Jacket'. In May 1295 the Scottish bishops, earls and barons elected a Scottish Council to govern instead of the vassal king. The Council negotiated an alliance with France against Edward and, in the name of King John, called all free men to take up arms against the English, a call ignored by the Bruce family.

The Scots ravaged northern England and attacked Carlisle, defended by the Bruces. Edward's army sacked the town of Berwick and marched into Scotland, taking over its castles one by one. John Balliol surrendered to Edward, who now had complete power in Scotland.

KING ROBERT BR
MARIIT ISSOBELI
TO THE ERLL (

JOHN BALLIOL PAYS
HOMAGE TO EDWARD
*On 26 December 1292,
John Balliol paid homage
for the kingdom of
Scotland to Edward I of
England. In spite of the
Treaty of Birgham,
Edward I claimed over-
lordship of Scotland.*

Comet le grante pouple bataillerent acontre le iour de iugemet par orgiul z par emuie par couetise.

Comet le comoune genz checon leial acotre autte uou   dia autte octite p le atiel pirinet
crise. Ecoo est dunt tious esproiuf been q le iour de dreiz iugemet for inet aproche.

THE SACK OF BERWICK
Edward led his army into Berwick on 30 March 1296 and ordered that its citizens — men, women, children, young and old — be slaughtered without mercy. The killing went on for two days before Edward called a halt.

CHTER
AR

FIRST MARRIAGE
In 1295 Robert the Bruce married Isabella, the daughter of the Earl of Mar, who had lands along the coast of Inverness. The marriage was tragically short, however, since Isabella died the following year, giving birth to a daughter, Marjorie.

EDWARD I
Edward I was one of England's most able kings. A contemporary wrote, 'He

is valiant as a lion, quick to attack the strongest … But … he is a panther in fickleness and inconstancy, changing his word and promise … The path by which he attains his ends, however crooked, he calls straight and whatever he likes he says is lawful.' Edward's ruthless treatment of the Scots earned him the epitaph, Scottorum Malleus *('The Hammer of the Scots').*

THE ARMIS OF THE BALLIOVN

BALLIOL DISGRACED
On 8 July 1296 John Balliol was forced to resign his kingdom to Edward, who stripped him of all his royal and heraldic insignia before imprisoning him in the Tower of London. He is shown here with his symbols of kingship torn and broken.

William Wallace

ALTHOUGH EDWARD was satisfied that Scotland was in his grip, bands of rebels and outlaws, who had taken refuge in the Scottish mountains and forests, began to attack the English. They were led by William Wallace and Andrew Moray, and the more success they had the more people flocked to join them, including Sir William Douglas. To quell the rebellion, Edward ordered the Governor of Carlisle to send his son, Robert, to attack the Douglas Castle.

As Bruce rode north with his men he was deeply disturbed. To whom did he owe his loyalty – to Edward or to Scotland? Douglas had supported his family's claim to the throne and Balliol was now in prison. By the time he reached the Douglas Castle he had come to a decision. He offered his men a choice: either stay with him and fight for Scotland, or return home.

Bruce gathered a large force from his own lands in Carrick and joined the rebels at Irvine. By August 1297 most of the area north of the Firth of Forth was under Scottish control. Then Wallace confronted the English army at Stirling Bridge in his first open battle. Although less well-equipped and far outnumbered, the Scots routed the English forces. As Edward's army retreated, Wallace became Guardian of Scotland and ruled in the name of King John.

His rule was short, however. In July 1298 the Scots again faced the English army at Falkirk, and this time the English made no mistake: their longbowmen wreaked havoc on the Scottish ranks. Wallace and the other survivors fled into the forest; faith in him fled too and the Guardianship of Scotland passed to Robert the Bruce and John Comyn. But these two were old enemies – Comyn was John Balliol's nephew. Bruce was again thrown into confusion about where his loyalties lay. Rather than accept Balliol's claim to the throne, he surrendered to Edward in 1302.

WILLIAM WALLACE
When Wallace embarked on his fight against the English, he had neither a title nor land. Until Sir William Douglas joined him, his followers were mainly common people intent on driving the English out of Scotland. This 19th-century painting of Wallace is by David Scott.

BATTLE OF STIRLING BRIDGE

Wallace used clever military tactics to beat the superior English forces at Stirling Bridge: as the English cavalry crossed the narrow bridge, Wallace cut them off from the rest of the army and defeated them.

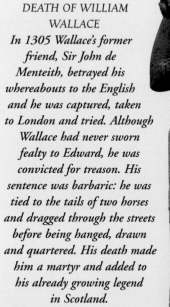

BRUCE'S SECOND MARRIAGE

In 1302 Robert the Bruce married Elizabeth de Burgh. Her father, the Earl of Ulster, was one of Edward's most loyal supporters, and the couple married soon after Bruce surrendered to Edward.

DEATH OF WILLIAM WALLACE

In 1305 Wallace's former friend, Sir John de Menteith, betrayed his whereabouts to the English and he was captured, taken to London and tried. Although Wallace had never sworn fealty to Edward, he was convicted for treason. His sentence was barbaric: he was tied to the tails of two horses and dragged through the streets before being hanged, drawn and quartered. His death made him a martyr and added to his already growing legend in Scotland.

THE BATTLE OF FALKIRK

Wallace was decisively beaten at Falkirk and up to 15,000 Scots were killed. Wallace never surrendered to Edward as Bruce did, but spent the rest of his life as a guerilla fighter and outlaw.

King But No Country

THE DEATH of Robert Bruce's father in 1304 opened the way for Bruce to claim the Scottish throne on the same grounds as his grandfather 12 years before. His greatest rival was Sir John Comyn, John Balliol's nephew, whom many thought had the greater claim, since, unlike Bruce, he had never swerved in his opposition to Edward. To win Comyn over, Bruce suggested a deal: either Comyn would become king and assign all his lands to Bruce or, if Bruce became king, Comyn would receive all his lands. Comyn accepted the latter proposal, but in 1305 he revealed the agreement to Edward.

Bruce learned of Comyn's betrayal in January 1306, when he narrowly escaped being arrested by Edward for treason. Bruce asked Comyn to meet him in Greyfriars Church in Dumfries and confronted him with his treachery. Daggers were drawn and Bruce stabbed Comyn to death under the high altar – a sacrilegious act. The Scottish bishops, who had never ceased to support Scottish independence, quickly absolved Bruce of his sin – although the Pope later excommunicated him. Many joined Bruce's banner and, on 25 March 1306, Bruce was crowned king in the abbey at Scone.

Edward was incensed when he heard the news and sent a large army north. Bruce's force was decimated by the Earl of Pembroke at Methven near Perth: those who were captured were savagely executed, while Bruce, his remaining followers and his family took refuge in the mountains of Atholl. They stayed on the mainland for several months living a dangerous life as outlaws, until Bruce decided they must seek safety. He sent his family first to Kildrummy Castle then to the Orkney Islands. He and his men moved south-west to Dunaverty Castle on the Mull of Kintyre and then on to Rathlin Island off the Irish coast. Their situation was now desperate, but Bruce never ceased to encourage his men and keep their spirits high.

CORONATION OF KING ROBERT I
Since Edward I had already removed the Stone of Destiny and the Scottish crown to Westminster, Robert the Bruce was crowned at Scone with a simple gold circlet. Thereafter Bruce never wavered in his fight for Scotland's independence.

AYMER DE VALENCE,
EARL OF PEMBROKE
The Earl of Pembroke, who led a large force against Bruce in 1306. Knowing Pembroke's reputation for chivalry, Bruce issued the Earl with a personal challenge to fight or surrender. Pembroke accepted the challenge for the following day, but at dusk treacherously took Bruce's men by surprise as they camped near Methven.

KILDRUMMY CASTLE

Kildrummy Castle in Moray was Bruce's stronghold in the north-east and the intended refuge for his wife, daughter and sisters as they fled to the Orkneys. On learning that the English intended to besiege the castle, however, Bruce's brother Nigel returned to Kildrummy without the women. The English eventually took the castle and Nigel was executed.

RATHLIN ISLAND

Just six months after being crowned king at Scone, Bruce landed on the island of Rathlin. His kingdom in English hands and his force much diminished, Bruce spent the winter of 1306/07 raising support in the western islands of Scotland.

SCONE PALACE

The traditional place of inauguration (or coronation) of Scottish kings is now in the grounds of Scone Palace. Having made his peace with the Church after the murder of Comyn, and having received oaths of fealty from many Scottish lords, Bruce rode straight to Scone.

SAVAGE PUNISHMENT

While fleeing to safety, the Queen and her party were taken captive at Tain and sent to England. The punishments Edward ordered for Bruce's sisters were bizarre and humiliating even for the time: they were each held for four years in solitary confinement in cages open to public view. Bruce's 12-year-old daughter was imprisoned in the Tower of London, and the Queen was held in a royal manor, without clothes, bed or other furniture.

Guerilla War

BY FEBRUARY 1307 Bruce was ready to reclaim his country. With a few hundred men, he set sail from the island of Arran to Turnberry in Carrick, where he raided the English soldiers while they slept unguarded. As soon as Edward heard that Bruce had invaded the mainland he poured troops into south-west Scotland.

Knowing that he did not have the resources to confront the well-equipped English soldiers head-on, Bruce took to the hills and waged guerilla war instead. Hiding in the familiar countryside of his childhood, he ambushed, raided and attacked small groups of the enemy. The more success he had, the more men dared to defy the English and join his cause. One day Christian of Carrick, a relative of Bruce, arrived at his camp with 40 soldiers, but she also brought the devastating news of the fate inflicted on his wife and family by Edward I. Grief-stricken, Bruce became more determined to succeed.

His first large-scale success was against the Earl of Pembroke (who had defeated him at Methven) at Glen Trool. From there, with ever-growing support, Bruce moved north into Ayrshire, but Pembroke followed and the two armies met again in May 1307 at Loudon Hill. Here Bruce's brilliant military tactics trapped and defeated the English.

Edward I had vowed to destroy the King of Scots, but he died in July 1307 near Carlisle. Bruce was overjoyed, especially when Edward II withdrew his soldiers from Scotland, except for those garrisoned in castles, to deal with trouble in England. Bruce seized the opportunity to take on the Comyn family and those Scots who opposed him. He and his supporters defeated these rebel lords one by one, until, by March 1309, Bruce controlled two thirds of the country. He held a parliament at St Andrews on 17 March 1309, the first free parliament in Scotland for 18 years and a sign to the world that Robert the Bruce was king of an independent nation.

GLEN TROOL
Bruce's first major success against the English was at Glen Trool in Galloway. Pembroke discovered that Bruce was camped there with 300 men and planned to take them by surprise, but Bruce learned of his presence and chased Pembroke and his 1,500 men out of the glen.

BRUCE AND THE SPIDER
While Bruce and his men were fugitives and outlaws, they lived off the land, often hiding in caves like these on Arran. It is in such a cave that the myth of the spider is set: Bruce on the point of despair is said to have watched a spider as it tried to spin a web across the cave. Six times it failed before succeeding, inspiring Bruce to carry on and defeat the English.

CORONATION OF EDWARD II

When Edward II was crowned on 25 February 1308, he was already in trouble at home. The English barons resented his overt affection for Piers Gaveston, whom he had made Earl of Cornwall, and Edward was constantly preoccupied with defending his favourite until 1312 when, in the midst of civil war, Gaveston was seized and executed.

ST ANDREWS

This view of St Andrews in the 16th century shows many buildings, such as the cathedral and the bishop's castle, that would have been there when Bruce held his first parliament in the town in 1309.

LOUDON HILL

Loudon Hill overlooks a broad causeway nearly 500 metres wide. Bruce cut trenches along the causeway to make it narrower and waited on Loudon Hill for Pembroke's men. As the English knights charged onto the causeway, they were thrown into confusion by the trenches and routed by the smaller Scottish force.

Bruce's Scotland

WITH THE holding of his first parliament at St Andrews, Bruce showed that he was now the effective king of most of Scotland, but what was this country like that he had striven so hard to gain?

The recognized borders were much the same as they are today, but the land was wild and mostly uncultivated, with misty moors, mountains, swamps and thick, dark pine forests, inhabited by wolves and wild boars. Deep ravines and glens, however, provided excellent cover and refuge for Bruce's guerilla army. Travel across country was difficult: the few tracks were usually too rough and muddy for wheeled transport, and in winter packhorses were often bogged down in mud or snow. Communications were mainly north–south along the coasts and up and down the navigable rivers. Before the ravages of the long war with England, the east-coast towns of Berwick, Edinburgh, Dundee, Perth, Aberdeen and Inverness had been flourishing ports with large populations of foreign merchants, trading with Germany, France, Scandinavia and the Low Countries. But the war destroyed this lucrative trade.

At the beginning of the 14th century, Scotland's population was much smaller than today's – fewer than 500,000 people. Apart from Norsemen in Caithness, Sutherland and the Western Isles and Anglo-Saxons in Lothian, most Scots were Celts. The Celts were traditionally grouped in large clans of loosely related families bearing the same name and owning large tracts of land. The MacDoualls, for example, ruled in western Galloway, the MacDonalds in the Western Isles. Each clan was led by a chief, to whom the members owed unquestioning loyalty. Like the Bruces, many Norman knights had intermarried with Celtic families, so bringing together the clan and feudal systems. Bruce had to gain the loyalty of all the knights and chieftains before he could reign securely.

WEST HIGHLAND CHIEFTAINS
These effigies of Highland chieftains show the kind of armour worn by the soldiers from the Western Isles who initially formed the bulk of Bruce's men.

VICTORY AT LOCH AWE
This engraving shows Bruce in the Pass of Brander above Loch Awe in 1308. Here John of Lorn, a rebel lord, planned to ambush Bruce as he traversed the narrow pass with his men, but Bruce 'saw through their ploy and outwitted the men of Lorn.'

Threave Castle was built near Castle Douglas, in Galloway, by the son of one of Bruce's most loyal and courageous supporters – Sir James Douglas. Bruce rewarded his supporters by granting them land taken from those whom he defeated.

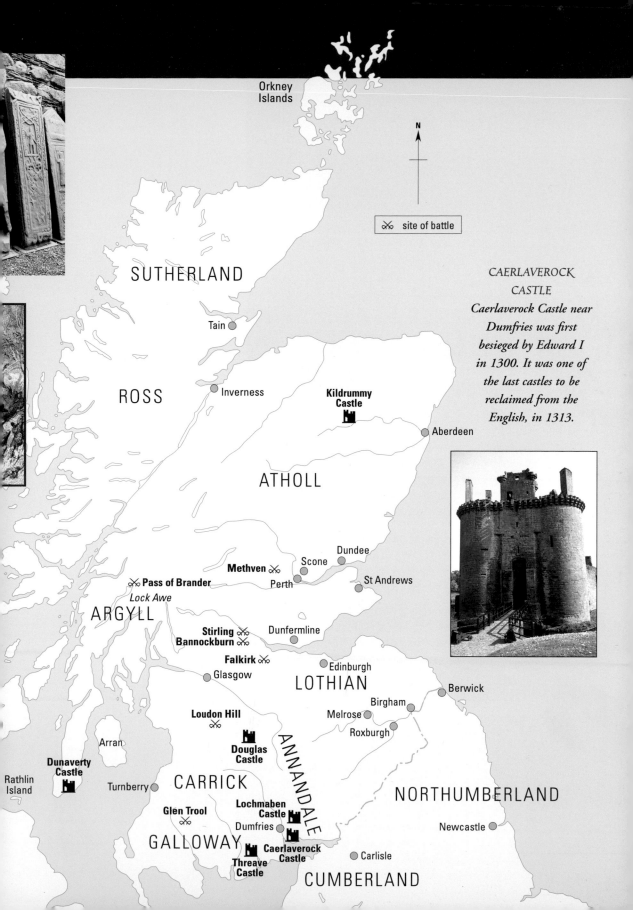

Orkney
Islands

N

⚔ site of battle

SUTHERLAND

Tain

ROSS

Inverness

Kildrummy
Castle

Aberdeen

ATHOLL

Dundee

Methven ⚔   Scone

Pass of Brander ⚔   Perth   St Andrews

Lock Awe

ARGYLL

Stirling ⚔
Bannockburn ⚔   Dunfermline

Falkirk ⚔

Glasgow   Edinburgh

LOTHIAN   Berwick

Birgham

Melrose

Loudon Hill   Roxburgh
⚔

Arran   Douglas
Castle   ANNANDALE

Rathlin   Dunaverty   CARRICK   NORTHUMBERLAND
Island   Castle   Turnberry   Newcastle

Lochmaben
Castle
Glen Trool
⚔   Dumfries

GALLOWAY   Caerlaverock   Carlisle
Threave   Castle
Castle   CUMBERLAND

*CAERLAVEROCK
CASTLE*
*Caerlaverock Castle near
Dumfries was first
besieged by Edward I
in 1300. It was one of
the last castles to be
reclaimed from the
English, in 1313.*

Path to Glory

SINCE 1290 Scotland had been devastated economically, but by 1311 England was in the middle of a civil war which King Robert used to his own advantage. He led his soldiers over the border into northern England, where he ravaged the countryside, seizing stores, arms, horses, and captives whom he held for ransom. Anyone who resisted was killed, but all others were spared. Durham, a wealthy town unprotected by Edward, offered Bruce £2,000 (about £1 million today) in return for ten months' truce. The people of Northumberland, Cumberland and Westmorland followed suit. Instead of wreaking slaughter and havoc, Bruce, the astute politician, used his power to improve his kingdom's finances: by 1314 he had collected more than £40,000 in tribute.

At the same time the Scots began to retake their castles. Using tactics and courage they often managed to avoid a long siege. In retaking the walled town of Perth, for example, Bruce waded at night through the icy waters of the moat with a ladder on his shoulders. Amazed at his audacity, his men followed suit and, setting the ladders against the wall, they climbed onto the battlements to take the town by surprise. In victory Bruce again showed political wisdom: he treated former enemies with humanity and leniency since it was more important to win their support than take revenge.

By March 1313 all the castles outside Lothian had fallen to the Scots except for Bothwell and Stirling. The success of these campaigns had rested on Bruce's strategy of avoiding open conflict with the superior English force. Then in the summer of 1313 Sir Philip de Mowbray, the commander of Stirling Castle, which was besieged by Bruce's brother Edward, offered to surrender if the castle was not relieved by midsummer 1314. Edward impetuously agreed, and so unthinkingly committed Bruce to the open conflict he had so long avoided.

CHARISMATIC LEADER
This portrait of Bruce was painted from imagination by George Jamesone in 1633. It nevertheless suggests his outstanding qualities of leadership, courage and humanity. Bruce was a personable, charming man who was popular with women as well as men: he fathered at least five illegitimate children!

STIRLING CASTLE
Stirling Castle, at the centre of Scotland, was too important strategically for Edward II to give up without a fight. When Mowbray offered to surrender the castle if it was not relieved, he knew that Edward would have to send an army to his aid – an army that Bruce knew he would have to intercept and defeat.

ROXBURGH CASTLE

Roxburgh Castle was retaken by James Douglas and his men in February 1314. Following Bruce's example, Douglas used stealth and tactics: draped in black cloaks to disguise themselves as cattle, his men crept up to the castle at night. They scaled the walls and took the English by surprise. Like other recaptured castles Roxburgh was razed to the ground to prevent it being reoccupied.

MOUNTED KNIGHT

This bronze figurine of an English knight was found in the River Tyne and dates from about 1300. He is clad in chain mail underneath a surcoat which showed his coat of arms. In battle the knight carried a battleaxe, a 12-foot (3.5-metre) lance, and a sword or mace. The horse too is protected by armour and by heavy blankets.

Battle of Bannockburn

SOME 2,500 English cavalry, 3,000 Welsh archers and 15,000 foot soldiers answered Edward II's call to arms and assembled near Berwick in June. From April 1314 Bruce had been assembling his army at Torwood, near Falkirk, and training his 5,000 to 6,000 soldiers. While Edward relied on his superior numbers, cavalry and weapons, Bruce carefully prepared his men and his tactics. Edward's army would advance along the old Roman road from Falkirk to Stirling across the Bannock Burn, so he ordered his men to dig pits beside the road. Then he laid out his troops in four groups, using the lie of the land to confine the vast English army into a limited space.

As the English marched from Edinburgh towards Stirling, Bruce moved among his men, many of whom he knew personally. On the morning of 24 June he addressed his troops: ' … be confident of success for we have right on our side … Think on your manhood and your deeds of valour and the joy that awaits you if you are victorious …'.

The Scots were indeed gloriously successful: the well-equipped English knights were put to flight by foot soldiers, the deadly Welsh archers were dispersed by Scots on horseback and the vast body of knights and soldiers were so penned in they could only fall back. Edward was forced to leave the battle and escape to England. At this point Bruce waved forward an array of camp followers, most of them unarmed, whom the English mistook for a second Scottish army. The English army's slow retreat became a panic-stricken flight.

Many English knights were taken captive, but Bruce ordered that they be treated as guests until their ransoms were arranged. The most illustrious, the Earl of Hereford, was exchanged for 15 Scottish captives, including Bruce's wife, daughter and Christina, his only sister still imprisoned. The English baggage train was captured and its contents distributed generously throughout Scotland.

FIGHT WITH DE BOHUN
One of the first English knights to reach Bannockburn on the eve of the battle, Sir Henry de Bohun spotted the Scottish king on his own sitting astride a pony. Seeking instant glory, he charged with lance drawn. Coolly, Bruce waited until the last moment, swerved and split de Bohun's skull with his axe.

THE BATTLE RAGES
This 19th-century mural of the Battle of Bannockburn was painted by William Hole. It shows Scottish foot soldiers slaying the English cavalry.

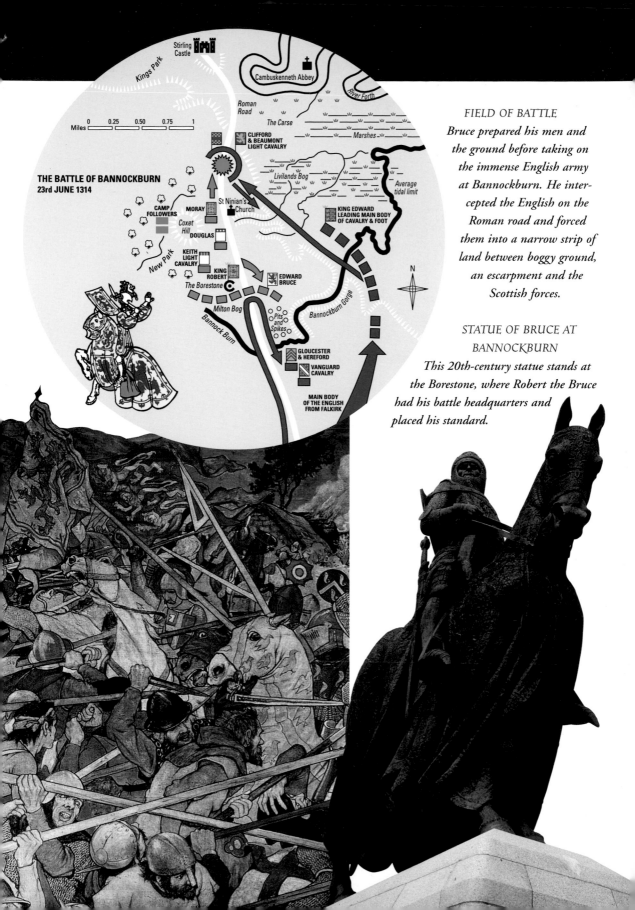

THE BATTLE OF BANNOCKBURN
23rd JUNE 1314

Stirling Castle
Kings Park
Cambuskenneth Abbey
River Forth
Roman Road
The Carse
Marshes
Miles 0 0.25 0.50 0.75 1
CLIFFORD & BEAUMONT LIGHT CAVALRY
Livilands Bog
Average tidal limit
CAMP FOLLOWERS
MORAY
St Ninian's Church
KING EDWARD LEADING MAIN BODY OF CAVALRY & FOOT
Coxet Hill
DOUGLAS
New Park
KEITH LIGHT CAVALRY
KING ROBERT
The Borestone
EDWARD BRUCE
N
Milton Bog
Pits and Spikes
Bannock Burn
Bannockburn Gorge
GLOUCESTER & HEREFORD
VANGUARD CAVALRY
MAIN BODY OF THE ENGLISH FROM FALKIRK

FIELD OF BATTLE

Bruce prepared his men and the ground before taking on the immense English army at Bannockburn. He intercepted the English on the Roman road and forced them into a narrow strip of land between boggy ground, an escarpment and the Scottish forces.

STATUE OF BRUCE AT BANNOCKBURN

This 20th-century statue stands at the Borestone, where Robert the Bruce had his battle headquarters and placed his standard.

Securing the Nation

THE BATTLE of Bannockburn left Bruce king of the whole of Scotland except for Berwick. He now had three main aims: peace with England, dependent upon Edward recognizing him as king of an independent Scotland; the lifting of his excommunication by the Pope; and an heir to his throne.

Like his father, Edward II refused to recognize Bruce as king, so to bring him to heel Bruce sent his troops into northern England where they raided, pillaged and exacted tribute. Edward did little to safeguard his people in the north, and in April 1318 the Scots recaptured Berwick. Edward could not accept the loss of such an important stronghold. In 1322 he amassed an army even bigger than that he took to Bannockburn and marched north. Bruce, however, again outwitted him, laying waste the land so that when the English army marched towards Edinburgh, they starved and were forced to retreat. It was Edward's last invasion of Scotland.

The Pope had continued to excommunicate Bruce and refused to recognize him as king of Scotland. In 1320 eight Scottish earls and 31 barons signed a document known as the Declaration of Arbroath. It was a moving and eloquent plea to the Pope to recognize the independence of Scotland and the legality of Robert the Bruce as king, but it took another four years before the Pope grudgingly addressed Robert as king of Scotland.

His family reunited after eight years in prison, Bruce was anxious to secure the succession to his throne. In March 1316 his daughter Marjorie, who had married Walter Stewart and become pregnant, was killed in a riding accident. Nevertheless she was delivered of a baby boy who was also called Robert. Then in 1320 Bruce's queen, Elizabeth, at last conceived and gave birth to a baby girl, followed in March 1324 by a son, David. At last Bruce had the heirs he needed!

THE DECLARATION OF ARBROATH
The Declaration of Arbroath is believed to have been written by Bernard Linton, Abbot of Arbroath and Chancellor of Scotland. It describes Bruce as king by common consent, who freed his people from the hands of the enemy, and ends with a promise of a crusade to the Holy Land if the war between England and Scotland is ended.

DRYBURGH ABBEY
The gable of Dryburgh Abbey is damaged by fire. Edward II gained nothing from his invasion of Scotland in 1322, but as he retreated he burned Dryburgh Abbey and sacked the abbeys of Holyrood and Melrose.

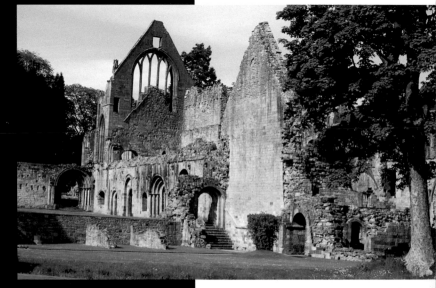

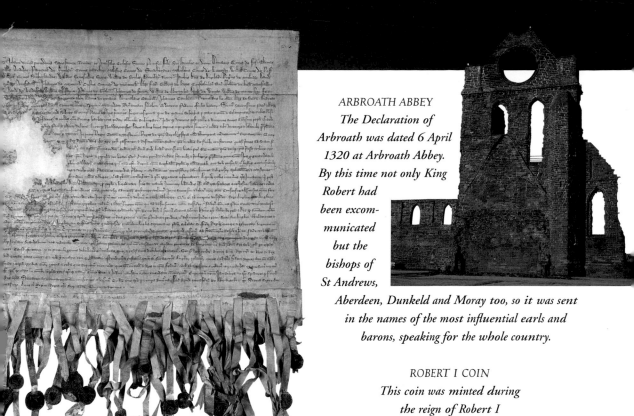

ARBROATH ABBEY
The Declaration of Arbroath was dated 6 April 1320 at Arbroath Abbey. By this time not only King Robert had been excommunicated but the bishops of St Andrews, Aberdeen, Dunkeld and Moray too, so it was sent in the names of the most influential earls and barons, speaking for the whole country.

ROBERT I COIN
This coin was minted during the reign of Robert I of Scotland.

SIR JAMES DOUGLAS RAIDING NORTHUMBRIA
The Scots continually raided northern England, burning towns, villages and crops before driving the sheep and cattle back to Scotland. Towns had to pay large tributes to preserve their homes and livelihoods.

BRUCE'S SEAL
The Great Seal of King Robert the Bruce.

Final Days

WHILE ROBERT the Bruce brought order and prosperity to Scotland, England was becoming increasingly chaotic. In 1327 Edward II was deposed by his queen, Isabella, and her lover, Sir Roger Mortimer. Edward's son was crowned Edward III a few months before Edward II was murdered. But Edward III was no more prepared to accept Bruce as king than his father had been, so Bruce sent his men once again to raid and pillage the north of England.

Unable to beat the Scots, Edward III sent two envoys to sue for peace in October 1327. Then he wrote letters in which he fully recognized the independence of Scotland and Bruce as king. He also agreed that his 6-year-old sister Joan should marry Bruce's 4-year-old son David. On 17 March 1328 Robert the Bruce with many of those who had fought alongside him for 30 years gathered at Holyrood to witness the sealing of the Treaty of Edinburgh, later ratified by Edward III at Northampton on 4 May. And in October 1328 the Pope at last removed the excommunication.

By now, Bruce, in his fifties, was infirm and increasingly unwell. Medieval writers referred to paralysis and leprosy but it is much more likely that he had suffered a stroke and scurvy. Unable to fulfil his promise to journey to the Holy Land, Bruce asked on his deathbed that his heart be taken there instead. Sir James Douglas, his companion in arms for so many years, gladly accepted the task. On 7 June 1329, Robert the Bruce, King of Scots, died and his body was buried in Dunfermline Abbey.

The following year, Douglas set out for the Holy Land, but while he was resting in Seville in Spain, the city was attacked by Moors. In the ensuing battle, Douglas was killed; his bones were taken back to Scotland and Bruce's heart was buried in the abbey at Melrose.

DUNFERMLINE ABBEY
After his heart had been removed, the body of Robert the Bruce was buried in Dunfermline Abbey, next to his wife Elizabeth, who had died in 1327, and among previous kings and queens of Scotland. The Scottish nation lamented the death of a heroic king and much loved man.

MELROSE ABBEY
After his death, Robert the Bruce's heart was embalmed and given to Sir James Douglas who carried it in a silver casket on a chain around his neck. When Douglas was killed in Spain, Sir William Keith of Galston carried Bruce's heart back to Scotland, where it was buried in Melrose Abbey.

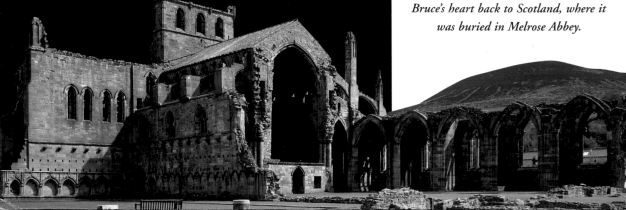